BUDDHA
OF INFINITE
LIGHT

BUDDHA

OF

*Revised with an Introduction
and Notes by*

TAITETSU UNNO

JILL KER CONWAY PROFESSOR
OF RELIGION AT SMITH COLLEGE

SHAMBHALA PUBLICATIONS

Boston & London · 1997

INFINITE LIGHT

D. T. Suzuki

in association with
THE AMERICAN BUDDHIST ACADEMY

Shambhala Publications, Inc.
Horticultural Hall
300 Massachusetts Avenue
Boston, Massachusetts 02115
http://www.shambhala.com

9 8 7 6 5 4 3 2 1

FIRST SHAMBHALA EDITION

Printed in the United States of America

⊗ This edition is printed on acid-free paper that meets
the American National Standards Institute z39.48 Standard.

Distributed in the United States by Random House, Inc.,
and in Canada by Random House of Canada Ltd

Library of Congress Cataloging-in-Publication Data

Suzuki, Daisetz Teitaro, 1870–1966
    Buddha of Infinite Light/D. T. Suzuki; revised with an
introduction and notes by Taitetsu Unno.
        p. cm.
    Rev. ed. of: Shin Buddhism.
    ISBN 1-57062-301-5
        1. Shin (Sect)—Doctrines.   2. Pure Land Buddhism—Doctrines.
    I. Unno, Taitetsu, 1929– . II. Suzuki, Daisetz Teitaro,
    1870–1966. Shin Buddhism. III. Title.
    BQ8718.7.s89 1998
    294.3'926—dc21   97-24078
                                                         CIP

CONTENTS

Foreword   7
Preface to the First Edition   9
Introduction   11

1. INFINITE LIGHT
   SHINRAN'S ORIGINAL INSIGHT   21
   THE TEACHING OF AMIDA   23
   PRIMAL VOW AND PURE LAND   26

2. ENLIGHTENMENT OF THE INNER SELF
   PRIMAL VOW OF AMIDA   29
   SINCERITY OF MIND   32
   THE STORY OF SHOMA   35
   OUR INNER SELF   37

3. FAITH AS TRUE ENTRUSTING
   SCIENTIFIC KNOWLEDGE   43
   BEYOND THE FIVE SENSES   46

Contents

DEEP SPIRITUALITY   48

ONENESS OF THE NAME   51

4. THE FUTILITY OF PRIDE

SELF-POWER AND OTHER-POWER   55

BEYOND SELF-POWER   58

MEANING OF NO MEANING   60

ISSA AND ECKHART   65

5. EXCELLENCE OF PERSON

MYOKONIN   69

LANGUAGE AND SPIRITUALITY   72

EVERYDAY LIFE AND NEMBUTSU   74

LIVING WITH AMIDA   77

EMBRACED BY NAMU-AMIDA-BUTSU   82

Notes   85

Suggested Reading   93

FOREWORD

This work is a completely revised edition of *Shin Buddhism* by D. T. Suzuki, first published by Harper and Row in 1970. The book was a transcription of a talk given by Suzuki in 1958 at the American Buddhist Academy in New York City. It contains a Preface by the Reverend Hozen Seki, founder of the Academy and resident minister of the New York Buddhist Church.

Some editorial work was essential in preparing this new English edition, due to flaws in the transcription, vagaries in some sections, and confusion in the order of some paragraphs. Part of the confusion arose from the fact that Suzuki used the blackboard to explain some concepts. This, of course, appears on tape as a disorganized, repetitive lecture. My revisions were aided immensely by the Japanese translation undertaken by Taira Sato and published in 1983 under the title *Shinshu Nyumon* by Shunjusha in Tokyo. Professor Sato prepared the translation by consulting the original tapes for chapters 1, 2, and 4 (none was found for chapters 3 and 5). His corrections and chapter subheadings have been incorporated into this new edition. I have also added an Introduction and Notes to provide a wider context for the main points made in the book. All this justified a new book title, *Buddha of Infinite Light*.

When D. T. Suzuki gave the lectures at the American Buddhist Academy, he was already eighty-eight years old and his audience probably had little or no knowledge of Pure Land Buddhism. I have tried to keep the unadorned style and informal nature of his talk. In spite of surface simplicity, the main teachings of Shin Buddhism are presented with sensitivity, clarity, and depth.

That this revised edition appears at this time is due to the efforts of several people working in concert. They include Hoken Seki and Brian Nagata of the American Buddhist Academy, Sam Bercholz of Shambhala Publications, and Wayne Yokoyama, who provided information on the Japanese translation. Credit is due to all of them for making this work possible.

TAITETSU UNNO
July 1, 1997

PREFACE
TO THE FIRST
EDITION

Where did I come from into this world?
Where am I going after death?

I CAME ALONE INTO THIS WORLD and am departing alone to the next world. If there were no compassion toward me from the Other-power, my past, present, and future would not exist. To protect and to guide me, there are countless powers. For example—my parents, my society, my nation, the air, earth, sun, etc.—all these powers of compassion are called *Oya-sama*. I cannot live in this world without Oya-sama. Oya-sama and I are in Oneness. Oya-sama is the infinite light and life that is called Amida Buddha.

In Japanese, *Namu* means "myself." NAMU-AMIDA-BUTSU is an expression of oneness—in other words, Oya-sama and I. Therefore when we recite NAMU-AMIDA-BUTSU it is an expression of gratitude for this universal compas-

9

sion that is always within us and surrounding us, regardless of whether we recognize or accept it.

We came into this world with Oya-sama and will return to Oya-sama after our death. Oya-sama is the source of joy, hope, and gratefulness.

Dr. Daisetz Suzuki, the world-renowned Buddhist scholar, presented a series of lectures on Oya-sama, a Japanese expression of great compassion that is also the Shinshu teaching, the truth of naturalness. The five lectures were sponsored by the American Buddhist Academy and taped in the spring of 1958 at the main hall of the New York Buddhist Church.

My dear friends Mr. and Mrs. Robert Blickenderfer, who had never met Dr. Suzuki or heard his lectures, were anxious to hear the tapes—they were greatly impressed and decided to transcribe the taped lectures for publication, in order that others too may enjoy the immensity of Dr. Suzuki's knowledge and wisdom on Buddhism.

Their great effort and patience have made this publication possible, for which I am deeply grateful.*

THE REVEREND HOZEN SEKI   •
Founder, American Buddhist Academy

---

*This Preface was written in connection with an earlier version that did not have the benefit of Professor Unno's scholarship. The corrections made for this revised edition do not lessen the generosity or dedicated labor of the original transcribers.

INTRODUCTION

B UDDHISM SPEAKS OF 84,000 PATHS to supreme
enlightenment. The number symbolizes the countless ways that can lead us to the world of liberation,
freedom, and peace. Among them is the Pure Land path,
prepared especially for ordinary mortals like you and me.
The significance of the number 84,000 is suggested in a
terse poem written by Saichi, a *myokonin*, or unlettered
but perceptive practitioner of Shin Buddhism.[1] In his
words:

> 84,000 delusions
> 84,000 lights
> 84,000 joys abounding

As long as our thoughts, feelings, and intuitions come
from a limited, finite, and karma-bound being, they are
all delusions. It is not a matter of right or wrong, good or

bad; this is our naked reality. They are delusions because they make us see the world from a deeply self-centered perspective—a fact that eludes our normal conscious awareness. Our myopic vision distorts reality; hence, our thinking, doing, and saying are invariably flawed and defective, even though we may not admit it. Religiously speaking, delusions arise from the darkness of ignorance (*avidya*), producing insatiable greed (*trishna*), and manifesting as blind passions (*klesha*). This is the cause of endless pain and suffering (*duhkha*).

The nineteenth-century thinker Friederich Nietzsche raised such an understanding to a philosophical level and characterized it as "perspectivism." From this vantage point he undertook a sweeping critique of existing moral values, religious teachings, and philosophical concepts as being without any objective foundations. In his *Will to Power*, he identifies the source of our delusions, and their expression in language, as follows:

> "Subject," "object," "attribute"—these distinctions are fabricated and are now imposed as a schematism upon all the apparent facts. The fundamental false observation is that I believe it is *I* who do something, suffer something, "have" something, "have" a quality.

Based on this fundamental error, we construct a world with words and concepts infused with our emotions. Our life, then, becomes filled with polarities, such as good and bad, like and dislike, love and hate, black and white, mine and not mine, enlightened and not enlightened, ad infinitum. Such is the world of 84,000 delusions.

We are made to acknowledge this life of fabrication when our reality is illuminated by light. This light focuses on each of the 84,000 delusions, making them transparent and powerless. Light is symbolic of wisdom in Buddhism, and this light is none other than the Buddha of Infinite Light (Amitabha). Since the light is not harsh, cold, and distant, but soft, warm, and proximate, it is felt as a compassionate working. Thus, the same Buddha is also called the Buddha of Infinite Life (Amitayus). In East Asia, the two are unified into a single name, Amida Buddha, and brought to life through the *nembutsu*, the uttering of NAMU-AMIDA-BUTSU.[2]

When we are made to see our delusions by virtue of compassionate light, we have been touched by reality. No longer are we lost or confused, afraid or angry, insecure or fearful—not because these states have vanished, but because they are revealed to us more clearly, securely cradled within the great compassion of the Buddha of Infinite Light. Each repetition of NAMU-AMIDA-BUTSU liberates us from our delusions, even as we remain karmically bound to them. This liberation—inconceivable, unexpected, and undeserved—is the cause for the endless celebration of this precious life: 84,000 joys abounding.

Such is the basic teaching of Shin Buddhism, which emerges from the rich and fertile ground of the Pure Land tradition with its 2,000-year history of cultivation by countless illustrious teachers. It will be helpful for us to briefly walk through this history, so that we can place this work in its proper context and appreciate its implications for our own times.

Pure Land Buddhism

The Pure Land tradition originated in India simultaneous with the rise of Mahayana Buddhism in the first century BCE. Historical evidence concerning the movement is obscure, but the scriptures of this tradition, later known as the Triple Sutras, appeared in the initial phase of the Mahayana movement. The Triple Sutras include two sutras of Indian origin, the *Larger Sukhavati-vyuha* and the *Smaller Sukhavati-vyuha*, both dating from about the first century BCE. The title means the "adornment" (*vyuha*) of the "land of bliss" (*sukhavati*), known more popularly as the Pure Land. We have extant Sanskrit texts and several Chinese translations. In addition, a third scripture, dating from about the fourth century, appeared somewhere in the Central Asian and northern Chinese cultural sphere. This is the *Sutra on the Contemplation on Amida Buddha*, which exists only in the Chinese version.

The basic message of the Triple Sutras centers on the Primal Vow, established by Dharmakara Bodhisattva, who upon its fulfillment became the Buddha of Infinite Light and Infinite Life, or Amida Buddha.[3] This mythic story of Amida and the Primal Vow originates before the beginning of human history, inspiring the life of the historical Buddha and successive masters of Buddha Dharma in East Asia. But it was not until the thirteenth century in Japan, during the Kamakura period, that the Primal Vow appeared on the center stage of history. The ripening of karmic circumstances, including sociopolitical disintegration, civil strifes and natural calamities, awareness of human finitude, and growing religiosity, prepared the way for the Primal Vow to become fully manifest and to play a crucial and lasting role in the life of the people.

Based on the teaching of the Triple Sutras, the cultic practices surrounding the Primal Vow eventually flourished as the Pure Land movement in China. By the fifth century CE more than two hundred Buddhist texts mentioned the name of Amida as the source of salvific power. Beginning with the White Lotus Society in the fourth century, different strands of Pure Land movements appeared in various parts of China. Among them, the most important for Japanese Pure Land is the lineage of T'an-luan, Tao-ch'o, and Shan-tao, preceded by Nagarjuna and Vasubandhu of India.

The Triple Sutras arrived in Japan together with the introduction of Buddhism in the sixth century, but they did not play a significant role of any kind in the early period. However, as the centuries passed, the Pure Land devotional practices attracted monks and nuns who could not find spiritual solace in existing practices. It also opened the gates of enlightenment to the general populace that had been excluded from the path. Although existing on the fringes of the major Buddhist schools, Pure Land became a powerful symbol of transcending this world of delusion, the realm of pain and suffering.

In the year 1175 the Tendai monk Honen, responding to the demands of a new age and the spiritual hunger of the people, proclaimed the establishment of an independent Jodo or Pure Land School. He advocated exclusive reliance on the Primal Vow of Amida Buddha, enacted by the constant saying of the name of Amida Buddha. This practice had been selected by the compassionate Buddha and granted to those who live in an age of decadence and turmoil. Unlike the established path of monastic Buddhism, which tended to be elitist, the Pure

Land path became the way of liberation and freedom for all people, regardless of class, age, gender, or even moral culpability.

Among Honen's disciples was Shinran (1173–1263), a relatively unknown Tendai monk, who abandoned the monastic life and devoted himself to following the path laid down by his teacher. In 1207 Honen and several of his disciples, including Shinran, were found guilty of inciting social unrest by preaching a new path and were exiled from the capital, Kyoto, to remote provinces. Shinran spent more than a quarter century in the outlying districts of northern Japan before returning to the capital.

Throughout his sojourn Shinran was in constant touch with people of the earth, the peasants and commoners. He continued to explore the depth of Honen's nembutsu teaching and over several years worked on the draft of his major opus, the *Kyogyoshinsho*, translated into English by D. T. Suzuki as *The Collection of Passages Expounding the True Teaching, Living, Faith and Realization of the Pure Land Way.* His sole intention was to clarify the working of great compassion as taught by Honen, defending his teaching against the criticisms leveled by the established schools. After his death, however, his followers founded a separate school, called Jodo Shinshu or Shin Buddhism, which eventually became the largest Buddhist school in Japan.

D. T. Suzuki

Daisetz Teitaro Suzuki was born in 1870 in Kanazawa, a stronghold of Shin Buddhism. In his autobiography he relates how he lost his father, a physician, while still a little boy, and how he therefore questioned the meaning of life at a tender age. His family came from a Zen background, but his mother was involved with a group that practiced an unorthodox form of Shin Buddhism current in the Kanazawa area.

Suzuki never completed his formal academic training but devoted his youthful years to Zen practice. In 1897 he came to the United States to work for Paul Carus of the Open Court Publishing Company through the intermediary of his Zen teacher, Shaku Soyen, who had participated in the Parliament of World Religions in Chicago in 1893. Suzuki lived in La Salle, Illinois, located far to the west of Chicago, until, in 1908, he left for Europe and eventually returned to Japan. At first he taught English at the Peers' School in Tokyo, but in 1921 he was invited to the faculty of Otani University, affiliated with the Higashi Hongwanji Branch of Shin Buddhism. Thus, although Suzuki's name is invariably connected to Zen, he did have a close relationship with the Shin tradition due to various external circumstances. But the much more compelling interest in Shin came from his own inner quest for religious awakening.

Throughout his life, Suzuki's primary concern was to explore and probe deep spirituality. He was a free spirit with an open mind, moving in multiple directions to satisfy this basic drive. Thus, he became engrossed with Swedenborg early in his career, wrote on Chinese philosophy, undertook English translations of the *Lankavatara* and the *Awakening of Faith in the Mahayana*, edited the *Gandavyuha*, undertook the study of Meister Eckhart, and discovered the world of Shin Buddhism.

Since Suzuki didn't come from the orthodox Shin tradition, his interpretation is not colored by sectarian dogma and sheds new light on its foundational experience. He was a pioneer in studying the writings of myokonin that had been neglected by orthodox Shin scholars. Among his posthumous works is a collection of the poems of the myokonin Saichi, who left more than ten thousand poems copied into more than thirty notebooks. Although he had little formal education, Saichi's poems reveal a spirituality unique in the literature of world religions.

When Suzuki speaks from the experiential standpoint about Amida, Pure Land, faith, and salvation, they take on a meaning that has universal implications. His subtle discussion of sincerity in religious practice and life is significant for both Buddhist and Christian spirituality. And his astute existential-psychological analysis of Shin faith underscores some shared commonalities with the Christian experience of grace.

Taitetsu Unno
May 1997

BUDDHA
OF INFINITE
LIGHT

1

INFINITE LIGHT

Shinran's Original Insight

THE PURE LAND TRADITION of Buddhism matured in China, but it accomplished its full development in the Shin school of Pure Land Buddhism. The Shin school is the culmination of Pure Land thought that took place in Japan. The Japanese may not have offered very many original ideas to world thought or world culture, but in Shin we find a major contribution that the Japanese can make to the world and to all other Buddhist schools. There is one other Buddhist school that originated in Japan—Nichiren. But all the other schools more or less trace their origin, as well as their form, to either China or India. Nichiren is sometimes confused with nationalism, but that is not its original intention. But Shin is absolutely free from such connections. In that sense, Shin is remarkable.

Shinran (1173–1263), the founder of the Shin school, lived in Kyoto, Japan. He is said to be of noble lineage, but that, I suspect, is fiction. He must have been more than just an ordinary person and probably belonged to a relatively cultured family, but he did not belong to the nobility. He might have had some connection with a noble family, but his training, his religious development, took place when he was exiled to the remote northern country, far away from the capital, the center of Japanese culture in those days. He was a follower of Honen, who founded the Pure Land school in Japan in 1175. Honen's influence was extensive at the time, and priests of the traditional schools were not pleased with his popularity. Somehow they contrived to have him and his followers, including Shinran, banished to the country.

Shinran's religious experience deepened during his period of exile. While living in the culturally deprived areas of Japan, he developed a profound understanding of the needs of the common people. In those days Buddhism was basically an aristocratic religion, and the study of Buddhism was confined to the learned class. Their approach was intellectual and rational, but Shinran knew that that was not the way to the authentic religious life. There had to be a more direct way, a religious experience that did not require the medium of learning or elaborate rituals. All such things had to be cast aside in order for one to have religious awakening. Shinran experienced this for himself, and he discovered the most direct way to that awakening.

Of all the developments that Mahayana Buddhism has achieved in East Asia, the most remarkable one is the Shin teaching of Pure Land Buddhism. It is remarkable because geographically its birthplace is Japan, and historically it is the latest evolution and the highest point reached in Pure Land Mahayana. The Pure Land ideas first originated in India, marked by the appearance of Pure Land scriptures probably about three hundred years after the time of the historical Buddha; that is, about one century before the Christian era.

In China the Pure Land movement took place toward the end of the fifth century, when the White Lotus Society was formed by Hui-yüan and his friends in 403 CE. The idea of a Buddha Land presided over by the Buddha is as old as Buddhism itself, but the tradition based on the desire to be born in such a land, in order to attain the final end of the Buddhist life, did not materialize until Buddhism flourished in China as a practical religion. It took the Japanese genius of the thirteenth century to further develop it in the form of the Shin teaching as we have it today.

Traditional Pure Land doctrine is quite heavily laden with all kinds of what I call accretions. These elaborations and appendages are not necessary for modern people to comprehend in order to get at the gist of the teaching.

The Teaching of Amida

Amida Buddha is the focus of the Pure Land teaching. He is depicted as being so many feet tall and endowed with all the admirable physical qualities of a great being. He emits light beams from his body, illuminating all the worlds—not just one world but the entire universe—so many worlds that it defies our human calculation of measurement. Every ray of light that comes out of his body, the pores of his skin, is a Buddha, amounting to countless Buddhas. These descriptions are extravagant, beyond human imagination.

This view, of course, is the product of human imagination, so I cannot say it is beyond it. But the ancient Indian minds are richly endowed with the ability to create fantastic imagery. Indians are the only people so extraordinarily gifted in that faculty. When you read the sutras and listen to the old ways of explaining Pure Land teaching, you are staggered at the disparity between the Indian interpretation and the modern way of thinking about such things. I am not going to go into the embroidered doctrines, so my explanation may seem somewhat prosaic and devoid of the glamour and rich imagery of the traditional Indian view.

Although Amida will be brought down to earth, the teaching is not to be treated from the intellectual standpoint or on the relative, earthly plane of thought, for it is altogether beyond human intellection. At the same time, however, Amida and Pure Land are revealed on this earth, but not as taught by orthodox teachers. The Pure Land is not many millions of millions of miles away to the West. According to my understanding, Pure Land is right here, and those who have eyes can see it around them. And Amida is not presiding over an ethereal paradise; his Pure Land is this defiled earth itself. It is now apparent that my Pure Land interpretation will go directly against the traditional or conventional view. But I have my own explanation, and perhaps my interpretation will lead you to agree with my views.

A friend in Brazil recently wrote to me, requesting that I write out the essential teachings of the Pure Land school in English, because it is difficult to translate Japanese into Portuguese. He wanted me also to present the doctrine in such a manner that it would emphasize its similarity to Christian theology, to show that Amida and Pure Land doctrine are at least superficially close to Christianity, yet retain their characteristic Buddhist features. So I sent him my explanation. Whether he agreed with it or not, I do not know. At any rate, I kept a copy for my own use, and I shall share parts of it with you.

First, I wrote that we believe in Amida Butsu, Amida Buddha, as savior of all beings. "Savior" is not a word that is normally used among Buddhists, and when it is used it is complying with Christian religious terminology. Amida Buddha is infinite light and eternal life. All beings are born in sin and burdened with sin. Of course, the idea of sin must be interpreted in the Buddhist sense of karmic evil.

Second, we believe in Amida Buddha as our *Oya-sama*, or *Oya-san*, as it is sometimes called. It is the term used to express love and compassion. *Oya* means parent, but not either parent, rather both mother and father; not separate personalities, but both fatherly and motherly qualities united in one personality. The honorific *san* is the familiar form of *sama*. The latter, *Oya-sama*, is the standard form. In Christianity, God is addressed as the Father—"Our Father who art in Heaven"—but Oya-sama is not in Heaven, nor is Oya-sama Father. It is incorrect to say "he" or "she," for no gender distinction is found. I don't like to say "it," so I don't know what to say. *Oya-sama* is a unique word, deeply endearing and at the same time rich with religious significance and warmth.

Third, we believe that salvation—"salvation" is not a good term here, but I am trying to comply with my friend's request—consists in saying the name of Amida in sincerity and devotion. Saying or pronouncing the name of Amida may not be considered important, but a name has certain magical powers, and when a name is uttered the object bearing the name appears before one. In *The Arabian Nights*, when the devil's name is pronounced, the devil appears. And among some people of earlier times the name of a god or supreme being is held sacred, revealed only to those initiates who have participated in certain rituals. The initiate is led by the elder of the religion into a dense forest, where there is no danger of being overheard by anyone. Then the elder tells God's name to the initiate. By knowing the name, the initiate is now fully qualified as a leader.

A name is highly significant in religious life. Amida's name is pronounced in sincerity and with devotion. The saying is NAMU-AMIDA-BUTSU. *Amida-butsu* is Amida Buddha. *Namu* expresses the taking of refuge. Thus, "I take refuge in Amida Buddha." It is a simple formula. There is nothing mysterious about it, and you may wonder how such a name, or such a phrase, could have such a wonderful power for all beings. But love and compassion are experienced when NAMU-AMIDA-BUTSU is pronounced with singleness of heart.

Primal Vow and Pure Land

I must now explain the Primal Vow of Amida. Primal Vow, according to my interpretation, is the primal will, and this primal will is at the foundation of all reality. Primal Vow, as expressed in the Pure Land sutra, is described by forty-eight aspirations, but they may all be summarized by one Primal Vow, which is simply this: *Amida wants to save all beings without exception.* Amida desires that all beings be brought to his land, the land of purity and bliss. And those who earnestly, sincerely, and devotedly believe in Amida will all be born in the Pure Land. The Pure Land is created for true and real followers, and it comes into existence when we sincerely intone NAMU-AMIDA-BUTSU.

This means that, instead of our going over to the Pure Land, it comes to us. In a way, we are carrying the Pure Land all along, and when we pronounce the Name, NAMU-AMIDA-BUTSU, we become conscious of the presence of Pure Land around us, or in us.

I need to explain the Primal Vow—or, in Japanese, *hon-gan*—in more detail. *Hon* means "original or primal," and *gan* means "vow, prayer, wish, or desire." More philosophically, it may be better to say "will," as in primal will. Why *will* is the preferred translation over *vow, prayer, wish, or desire* shall become clearer later.

Some people may wonder how the Mahayana could have evolved into the doctrine of Pure Land Buddhism. It apparently stands in direct contrast to the Buddha's supposedly original teaching of self-reliance and enlightenment by means of perfect wisdom (*prajna*).

Amida stands on one side, and on the other side stands ordinary people (*bombu*) like you and me. This relationship is also defined in terms of Amida as *ho*, in contrast to *ki*. These Japanese terms are difficult to translate into English, but *ho* is on the other side and *ki* on this side. *Ho* is Other-power, and *ki* self-power.[4] Christianity's

27

version of this contrast is between "God" and "sinful beings." Other-power and self-power stand in contrast: to be born in the Pure Land one must abandon self-power and embrace Other-power. In fact, when Other-power is embraced by self-power, self-power turns into Other-power, or Other-power takes up self-power altogether.

In a similar way, on one side we have Pure Land, and on the other side this world, called *shaba* in Japanese, from the Sanskrit *saha*. Shaba, we might say, is the realm of pain, the land of defilement, in contrast to the land of purity. Pure Land is the realm of the absolute, and this world the realm of relativity.

When we say NAMU-AMIDA-BUTSU, *namu* is self-power, or *ki*. *Amida-butsu* is Other-power, or *ho*. Thus, NAMU-AMIDA-BUTSU is the unity of *ki* and *ho*. This unification is the oneness of Amida and ordinary beings, Other-power and self-power, this world and Pure Land. So, when NAMU-AMIDA-BUTSU is pronounced, it represents or symbolizes the unification of the two. Unification is not an adequate term, but its meaning will become clear.

Now, Amida is on the other side and the bombu on this side; Pure Land on the other side and shaba on this side. Pure Land reveals itself when we realize what we are and where we are. Amida is also realized in the same way. When Amida and Other-power are understood, Pure Land will inevitably become significant too. When Amida's essential quality is comprehended, Primal Vow and compassion or love will also accompany it. It is just like grasping the central part of a piece of cloth. If you pull the middle up, all the rest comes with it.

2

ENLIGHTENMENT OF
THE INNER SELF

Primal Vow of Amida

AMIDA BUDDHA WAS ONCE a human being, but it is rather difficult to determine exactly how long ago. A long, long time ago, he was one of the sons of a great king. When he saw how miserable the human condition was, he wanted to extricate people from such a wretched existence and bring them to the Other Shore of the stream of birth and death. He was so compassionate that he felt all the sufferings of other people as if they were his own. His interest in the welfare of all beings was unstained by selfishness. It was altogether altruistic. Ordinarily, whatever interest we may take is grounded in self-interest. Some people go so far as to say that we are devoid of altruistic impulses, but I cannot agree with such views. We do have altruistic impulses and we often show evidence that we do. We forget ourselves and risk our

lives for others, and in pursuing that course of conduct we
don't think about anything. We do it impulsively, indicat-
ing that our actions arise from our fundamental nature.

Amida Buddha is shown to represent this altruistic impulse that is deeply rooted in human nature, perhaps rooted in the cosmos itself. This is why I speak of
the Primal Vow as being an expression of primal will. To
achieve altruism, according to the Indian way of thinking,
one must be purified of all defiled sentiments, feelings,
or emotions. Otherwise, one cannot expect to save others.
So Amida sought such a perfection.

Another idea generally held by Indian thinkers
and religious figures is that when one attains spiritual perfection, the place where one is situated, or one's environment, also changes. That is, when a person attains
enlightenment, or moral perfection, the environment in
which he or she exists also changes accordingly. When
Amida attained enlightenment, therefore, the environment changed in the same way. The country or realm
changed with Amida's enlightenment and became a place
conducive for other people to attain the selfsame enlightenment. Other people who come to that country, called
the Pure Land, will attain enlightenment without strug-
gling against great odds or obstacles.

When he was living as a human being, there was
a great Buddha from whom Amida wanted to receive enlightenment to make himself fit for the creation of an
ideal land. This Buddha made Amida see all the lands
from which he could choose, and Amida chose the Pure
Land. Some lands were not absolutely pure, some were
mixed with impurities and defilements, and the others
were not altogether desirable. Thus he chose the Pure

Land, where there was no stain of defilements or impurities.

Amida disciplined himself for many eons or *kalpas*. In the Indian tradition a *kalpa* is an extremely long period of time; in fact, it goes almost beyond human calculation. With enough patience, mathematicians might determine it, or modern machines might compute it, but it exceeds the imagination of ordinary people like ourselves. Amida trained himself morally by practicing the Six Perfections—generosity, discipline, perseverance, effort, meditation, and wisdom. Undertaking that practice for many kalpas, he finally attained enlightenment.

Before he attained enlightenment, he made a vow. In fact, he made forty-eight vows, but one of the vows is central, favored by the Shin people. Without this vow, the Eighteenth Vow, the other vows lose their miraculous powers of helping beings. This crucial vow is found in the *Large Sutra of Eternal Life*, and translated from the Chinese reads something like the following:

> If, upon my obtaining Buddhahood, that is, obtaining enlightenment, all beings in the Ten Quarters should not desire in sincerity and truthfulness to be born in my country, and if they should not be born there by only thinking of me for, say, up to ten times—except those who have committed the five grave offenses and those who are abusive of the true Dharma—may I not obtain the highest enlightenment.

Now, in this vow it is most important to have the desire to be born in Amida's country, not just superficially or lightheartedly, but in sincerity, in earnestness, most seriously and fully trusting in Amida's power to make us be born there. At the same time, one must pronounce the Name, NAMU-AMIDA-BUTSU. According to the Shin tradition, just one time is enough, but this sutra advises "up to ten times." In fact, pronouncing Amida's name just once is enough, but if once is enough, then ten times will also be sufficient. We might repeat his name many times, ever so many times, but we must pronounce the name in sincerity, really wanting to be born in his country. To be born in that country means to obtain enlightenment as Amida himself did. We cannot simply desire to be born into the Pure Land for the sake of happiness, because the object of being there is to attain supreme enlightenment.

Sincerity of Mind

We sincerely pronounce the name of Amida, fully trusting that his vow will enlighten us. To utter the name once with trustfulness and sincerity is enough, but generally we do not pronounce it sincerely. We may think that we are sincere and in possession of faith or belief in Amida, but real sincerity, real trust, is altogether devoid of such consciousness. As long as sincerity is conscious of itself, it is not genuine. So a sincere person does not say, "I am sincere."

Such an attitude, however, may remain just a little bit, unnoticeably or insignificantly, in the depth of the unconscious; although the unconscious cannot be conscious, something of consciousness stays submerged

there. And because that consciousness is left in the unconscious, it comes up sometimes unexpectedly, saying,
"Why, I am so sincere, and yet people don't believe me!"
When we feel this way, even when we are most sincere,
we are not being sincere at all.

When we say Amida's name while such con-
sciousness remains we cannot be born in the Pure Land.
Therefore, to pronounce NAMU-AMIDA-BUTSU is to forget
altogether, not to be conscious at all, of saying NAMU-
AMIDA-BUTSU. But when I identify myself with NAMU-
AMIDA-BUTSU and forget that I am the person saying the
Name, it is still not enough. Even when I feel that it is the
Name itself pronouncing itself, that NAMU-AMIDA-BUTSU is
pronouncing itself, it is not sincere if consciousness still
remains.

"Sincerity" is perfect forgetting of oneself, but at
the same time not just forgetting. In our ordinary life we
forget many things and do all kinds of things, but this is
not the forgetfulness referred to here. Religious or spiritual forgetfulness is something that one must experience
personally for oneself. That is, one has to experience it
personally to know what kind of forgetfulness or uncon-
sciousness we are talking about.

Now, with this vow we follow his words, or his
instruction, and in this way sincerity is obtained. Enlightenment then becomes a reality. But according to Shin
teaching, in this relative existence of ours, however sincere we might try to be, still a certain amount of insincerity is with us. It is inevitable. Relative existence and
insincerity are always inextricably related. Thus the inevitable conclusion: *as long as we live this human life, the attainment of perfect enlightenment is impossible.* If we go to

33

the Pure Land, however, where no stain of relativity, no defilement, exists, such remnants of relative existence will also be nonexistent. That is the most fit place for enlightenment to take place. This is the vow of Amida.

Finally, after undergoing disciplines and austerities for countless kalpas, Amida obtained enlightenment. In another part of the sutra Amida vows, "When I obtain enlightenment and all beings do not obtain enlightenment, may I not attain the highest enlightenment." Therefore his attainment of enlightenment is dependent upon our obtaining enlightenment. This may be quite difficult to understand. I leave much of it to the reader's own thinking, since, while it may appear lazy on my part, I think it is best.

Some people say, "Amida obtained enlightenment and has his own Pure Land—what's the use of our pronouncing his name and wishing to be born in the Pure Land?" The very fact that Amida obtained his enlightenment shows that we also have already obtained our enlightenment. We received it when Amida attained his so many kalpas ago. Thus we can say, "We are Buddhas from the very first, from the beginningless beginning of time. There is no need of our wishing to be born in the Pure Land or our pronouncing NAMU-AMIDA-BUTSU. Everything is done on the part of Amida, and we simply live just as we like."

But people who live like that, without having anything on their minds, without anxiety of any sort, exist like animals, like dogs or cats. Of course, they don't think about Amida, getting enlightenment, or being born in the Pure Land. If we could reduce ourselves into the same state—spiritually, mentally, and psychologically—as that of dogs and cats, it might be all right. In a way, dogs and cats are very much better than we are, although ordinarily we think that we're superior to them. Strangely enough, we are not content with the state in which we find ourselves; we are always discontented with our lives. There is a reason for this: our existence here on earth is really meant to be transcended. If in another realm we can discover the meaning of existence, the value of this life, the value of living here and now, that is what is most important. If we could realize the significance of life, the value of this very existence, then the end of living would be attained and we would have no more selfish desires.

The Story of Shoma[5]

I have been reading Meister Eckhart recently. When someone asks him, "What is eternal life?" he answers in one of his sermons, "Why not ask eternal life itself, instead of asking me?" If you want to know whether you can realize Buddhahood, you had better ask the Buddha himself. That is the way Eckhart answered.

This reminds me of a certain Shin layman in Japan some years ago. Although Shoma was an uneducated day laborer, he had a wonderful appreciation of the Buddha Dharma. It is marvelous that such an ignorant person can grasp the deepest possible meaning that even learned, scholarly, and acute-minded philosophers fail to grasp because it is too deep for their understanding. This unlettered but devout person understood Buddhism perfectly, and he was well known among his neighbors for his deep insight. Actually, his "neighborhood" extended many miles beyond his home, for numerous people living in faraway districts heard of Shoma's devotion and understanding. Thus they came from near and far to inquire of him about being saved, or being born in the Pure Land, or coming into touch with Amida.

One day a man began his journey from a distant place to see Shoma. In those days there were no trains or airplanes, so he had to walk several hundred miles for the visit. When he finally reached Shoma's place, he found him busily pounding rice for his day's wages. In ancient times—not so very ancient, since I still remember pounding rice myself—rice had to be refined by pounding it in a big wooden mortar with a pestle. It is rather hard work, but Shoma was busily engaged in it when the weary man finally arrived and asked him, "Pray, pray tell me, how can I be born in the Pure Land? How will Amida be gracious enough to look after me?"

Shoma did not answer, and just went on pounding rice without paying any attention to the visitor. But this man who had come from afar kept asking his question very earnestly. Still Shoma remained obdurate and did not even look at him. When the people who hired him saw this, they felt pity for the visitor and asked Shoma not to be so impolite and unconcerned. Yet he kept on pounding rice. The people invited the man into the house and offered him a cup of tea.

After some time had elapsed, the traveler, disappointed and despairing, said sadly, "I came such a long way, but if I can't get any answer concerning Amida and his salvation, I can do nothing but go home to my native town." He looked miserable. As he was about to depart,

Shoma said, "If you are in such a desperate state of mind, you are altogether wrong in asking me about such things. Why don't you go to Amida-sama himself? He is the one who deals with such questions. It's none of my business." The traveler left, deeply touched by this thought.

Voltaire is quoted as saying, "To save people is divine business, the business of God, and we don't have anything to do with it. Leave that to God; we don't have to bother with that kind of thing. We shouldn't interfere with God's business." If Voltaire really said that, he was a great spiritual person, an enlightened man like Shoma. I do not know whether Voltaire was such a highly spiritual person. That's another matter. But if we take these words just as they are, Voltaire is quite right, just as Shoma was right.

You may feel that we do not have anything to do with Amida, that Amida is extraneous to our lives, a kind of being who occasionally or sporadically or even erratically comes into our lives, as Christians would say, "by divine grace." Divine grace appears randomly in our lives so that we cannot depend on it all the time.

Our Inner Self

What kind of being is Amida? My understanding about Amida is that the *Larger Sukhavati-vyuha Sutra*, which describes his vows and enlightenment, is basically mythical in the sense that it is telling a story that transcends history, which is bound by time. It has almost nothing to do with so-called conventional history.

I remember talking many, many years ago to an American philosopher who was visiting Japan, James Bissett Pratt, who is no longer living.[6] He had a very good understanding of Buddhism. Dr. Pratt and I were discussing the Christian emphasis on historical fact and how Christianity depends on history. Buddhism, on the other hand, ignores what is known as objective history and relies more on the legendary and the mythical.

We came to and agreed on the following: myth, legend, and tradition ("tradition" may not be the proper term) and poetical imagination are actually more real than what we call factual history. What we call facts are not really facts—not so dependable and not so objective as that word implies. Objectivity in the true and real sense is found in religious myth, poetic and metaphysical truth. So we concurred that the story of Amida has more objective and spiritual reality than mere historical truths. Amida is really ourselves—this is the reason that we can accept the story of Amida so readily and understand the story of Shoma and other devotees of the Shin tradition.

In the story itself is something very deep which directly appeals to our innermost mind. We can say that there is outer mind and inner mind. We generally lean on this outer mind or outer self, not the inner or inmost self. The inmost self lies deeply buried in the unfathomable abyss of our relative consciousness. This self is ordinarily well concealed under layers of all kinds of things moving on the surface of consciousness. The latter is what we generally take as the real self, but actually it is not. The real inner self is difficult to awaken. And to awaken that inner self, according to Shin doctrine, one pronounces the name of Amida, NAMU-AMIDA-BUTSU. But merely to say

NAMU-AMIDA-BUTSU will never awaken the inner self. As I have said, NAMU-AMIDA-BUTSU is to be pronounced with sincerity and real devotion. Our outer self, which is superficial, works on the surface of our consciousness. This superficiality consists in bifurcation. When we think, "This is my self," or "This is my inner self," that self is already divided into two—the self and something that stands against that self. When we become conscious of ourselves, we always have the one who thinks and the one who is thought—subject and object. Subject and object are always present in our consciousness.

The *Dhammapada*, one of the earliest texts of Buddhism, discusses at great length the destroying of consciousness, or getting rid of consciousness. When people read a phrase like "the destroying of consciousness," they assume it means negating human existence altogether, that it is like committing suicide. This is the gospel of negativity Westerners often criticize. Asians, then, are accused of being life negating. But actually "the destroying of consciousness" means destroying the superficial, relative consciousness. It means going beyond the bifurcation of subject and object.

Subject and object, before they split, emerge from where there is no subject or object yet. This world that we take for granted and see is intellectually reconstructed; it is not the real one. We have re-formed it through our senses and our intellect working at the back of the senses. We reconstruct this world and believe that our fabrication is the real thing.

But to reach the inner self, such superficial relativity must be eradicated. To destroy relativity is not to create another relativity, but to find relativity itself as un-

divided into relative terms—which, again, is rather difficult to understand. But the inner self is reached only
when this relativity is transcended. When there is no subject and no object, some Buddhists would say, we are in
a state like that before we were born into this world. We
see things as we did before we came into this world.

But to talk this way we usually have to use language, and language always works in time. Therefore, everything we verbalize is chronologically ordered. So I say,
"before I was born," or "the state I was in before I came
into this world." All such phrases refer to actions which
took place in the past. They are conditioned by time. Our
language itself is hampered with this dualism. So when I
speak of transcending this attitude of relativity, what do I
mean? We can't think; we can't ever bring it to consciousness.

Consciousness itself is a product of time. Thus,
to destroy that product of time and yet to reproduce it in
time, to destroy consciousness which is in time and yet to
have whatever experience we get by it, seems contradictory. Such an experience expresses itself through consciousness, in consciousness, *in terms of time.* That which
goes beyond time we try to express in time. This is a
contradiction as long as we appeal to language, but we
have no alternative but to appeal to language. So we are in
a constant dilemma; we have to live with that somehow.

And then we know that our real, inmost self is
where subject and object have not made their appearance. It is as if the world had not yet come into existence.
You may ask, "What was there before the world came
into existence?" Such a question simply reveals thought
patterns conditioned by time. My answer to it would be

that before the world came into existence is this present moment, this absolute moment. Metaphysically speaking, such a moment is the time we really experience sincerity, the time we experience what Christians would call "forsaking the self." Forsaking self is forsaking relativity of self and getting into the inmost self, which knows no subject, no object, no sincerity, no insincerity. When we are conscious of sincerity we are generally also conscious of insincerity, for they are involved with each other. When sincerity and insincerity are transcended, then Amida comes into our inner self and identifies himself with this inner self. Or, we can say, this self finds itself in Amida. And when we find this self in Amida, we are in the Pure Land.

As I said before, we don't go out of this world in order to be born in the Pure Land, but we carry the Pure Land with us all the time. Being born in the Pure Land means discovering the Pure Land in ourselves. We never seem to realize that. Ordinarily we tell people, "If you do something bad, you will surely be destined for some undesirable place. But if you behave yourself, you will be born in the Pure Land. How happy you will be!"

In Japanese, and perhaps in Chinese, we have a saying: "Give a child a yellow leaf, and he will play with it as if it were real gold." We play with yellow leaves, thinking that they are valuable. In fact, we play with yellow leaves a great deal. How guileless we are! To believe in a Pure Land after death is like playing with yellow leaves as if they were gold.

We find our inner self when NAMU-AMIDA-BUTSU is pronounced once and for all. My conclusion is that Amida *is* our inmost self, and when that inmost self is found, we are born in the Pure Land. The kind of Pure Land located elsewhere, besides where we are, is most undesirable. What is the use of lingering in the Pure Land, enjoying ourselves and doing nothing? Most people don't think about that, and it's a good thing. If they thought about it they would become dissatisfied with themselves and get themselves into trouble. It is better not to think of those things.

God seems cruel to put us human beings into this world of birth and death, making us suffer so much. But nothing awakens religious consciousness like suffering.

3

FAITH AS TRUE
ENTRUSTING

Scientific Knowledge

HUMAN BEINGS FIND NAMES ESSENTIAL.
Names are discriminating; they distinguish one
thing from another. By distinguishing one object
from another object, we are aided in understanding the
world. If we did not know the nature of an object to which
we have given a specific name, it could not be distinguished from another object. Therefore, discrimination is
essential to understanding objects. But names are not everything.

Another unique aspect of human beings is this:
people by nature manufacture all kinds of tools. Names
are also tools. With names we handle objects. But invent-
ing tools may lead to the "tyranny of tools." When tools
become tyrannical, instead of our making use of them,
they rebel against their inventors and take revenge. Then

43

we are made tools of the tools that we make. This strange process is especially noticeable in modern life. We invent many machines, which in turn control human affairs, our human life. Machines, especially in recent years, have inextricably entered our life. We try to adjust ourselves to the machine, because the machine refuses to obey our will once it's out of our hands.

In our intellectual processes, ideas can also be despotic, for we cannot always control the concepts we use. We invent or construct many ideas, many concepts. They are very useful to us in dealing with our life, but convenient ideas frequently control their inventors and become despotic. Scholars who invent ideas forget that they formulated them in order to handle realities for a specific purpose. Each science, whether it is called biology or psychology or astronomy, works with its own premises and its own hypotheses. Each science organizes the field it has chosen—whether it be stars, animals, fish, and so on—and works with those realities according to the conceptual scheme especially devised to study them for our understanding. In pursuing their theories and using their formulations, scientists sometimes find themselves in situations that cannot be explained by their concepts. Then, instead of dropping those ideas and trying to create new concepts so that the unexpected difficulties can be included and handled, they often stick to the first ideas that they have devised and try to make the new realities obey those ideas. Or they simply exclude anything which cannot be covered by the network of ideas they have created.

You might say that some scientists catch fish in a net with certain standardized meshes. Those fish that cannot be scooped up and captured in the net will be dropped—they won't be considered worth saving. The scientist-fishermen just take up those that can be caught in their net and try to explain their catch by means of the ideas they already possess. Other fish are considered not to exist. The person holding the net says, "These fish exist, caught in my net. All others don't exist."

The example can be extended to astronomy. When stars do not come into the scope of an existing telescope, those stars are neglected. The invention of a very powerful telescope would enable the astronomer to survey the sky more widely and more extensively. But when some astronomers are asked about those parts of the universe which cannot come into the scope of existing telescopes, they shrug them off as unimportant. Sometimes they even go so far as to say that space is empty beyond a certain group of stars. Certain galaxies make up their astronomical maps, and beyond that there is said to be a void.

Such conclusions are altogether unwarranted. If scientists were content with reaching conclusions on what they can survey or measure, that would be all right. If they maintain that beyond that they do not know and don't venture any theory or hypothesis, that is also all right. But sometimes blinded by their own brilliance, by whatever success they have already achieved within certain boundaries, they try to extend that achievement beyond the established boundaries, as if they had already surveyed and measured that which is beyond what they already know. That is the trouble with some scientists.

Now, the problem with ordinary people is that they blindly rely on what scientists say. But scientists must always make conditional statements, for they all begin with certain hypotheses. When scientists could not explain light, for example, they invented what they call "wave theory." But the wave theory did not account for all phenomena connected with light, so scientists introduced "quantum theory." This made the explanation of other phenomena possible, but then scientists discovered that in order to explain all phenomena they had to use *both* theories. Unfortunately, the two theories contradict each other, so that when the wave theory is adopted quantum theory must be thrown out. And when the quantum theory is utilized the other theory must be discarded. But certain phenomena exist, and scientists cannot deny their reality. Thus, however contradictory they may be, both theories have to be adopted. Somehow they have to coexist.

Beyond the Five Senses

Furthermore, we have the five senses, and our knowledge of reality is connected with them. If we had another sense, or two or three more senses beyond the existing five, we might find something altogether different existing. If we say that our five senses exhaust reality, that is presumptuous on our part. We can say, however, that as far as our five senses and our intellect are concerned the world is to be understood, explained, and interpreted in a certain way. But there is no way to deny the existence of something (it may or may not be proper to speak of "someone") higher or deeper, something that covers the field more extensively. There may be something beyond the measure of our five senses and our intellect. We may possess some such thing in ourselves, perhaps largely underdeveloped. If we have another way of coming into contact with reality that is much deeper, more extensive, than our senses and intellect permit, it is presumptuous of us to deny such an intuition, and claim, "There is no such thing—nothing exists outside my senses and intellect."

We are arrogant if we deny this higher and deeper intuition, which in Pure Land Buddhism is the *myogo*, "the Name." The working of this Name allows us to enter the Pure Land and makes possible our realization of the highest reality, a full grasp of ultimate truth. It does not work on our senses and intellect, which are limited and relative. People who hold the intellect to be our only real guide in life will deny that which extends beyond the senses and intellect. They will negate the efficacy of the Name to explore those fields of human life that cannot be grasped by intellection.

Religious life is characterized by an experience peculiar to it, called faith. Faith is quite a strange and wonderful thing. Ordinarily, when we speak of "faith" or "belief," we refer to something beyond our everyday comprehension. Religious faith means that we reach a point where we have to venture into that life opened up by faith. In conventional life what we might call relative faith insists, "Unless I have seen it or unless I have heard it myself personally, I cannot believe it."

When we accept any statement communicated to us by our friends or books or other sources, because we judge that the source of the statement is reliable, we think it is true, taking it for granted that the evidence

47

is strong enough and can be verified. Even though the evidence is outside of our personal experience, we believe or have faith in it. But in religious faith there is something more than that.

Even when our intellect is unable to verify what scientists call objective or scientific truth, there is something in religious faith that somehow we must accept as reality. Although we have yet to experience it, and we probably may never experience it, still it demands our acceptance, whether we will or not. This is the manner in which theologians speak of faith. One must make a decision to accept it or not to accept it. It is a venturesome deed or experience, plunging oneself into an unknown region and risking one's destiny. But I am afraid that people who have such a view of faith are still on the plane of relativity.

The fact is that we are compelled to act—it is not a matter of choice that we accept faith. All religions contain a similar element. It is not that Amida enters our life in some way; rather, our being is carried away by Amida. That is the way that the Name comes alive in the actual life of a Shin Buddhist. Some people may ask about the significance of the Name and how it can be so efficacious as to carry us to Amida and the Pure Land. As long as a person has such doubt or question or hesitancy in accepting the Name, he or she is not yet in it, and therefore cannot fully experience it.

Deep Spirituality

In India there is a mythical bird called the Garuda, a golden-winged bird. In the sutras it is described as being huge; for food it eats dragons who live in the ocean depth. When the golden-winged bird up above detects the dragons at the bottom of the ocean, it swoops down from the sky. The waves open up, and the bird picks up the dragons from the deep to devour them. The dragons, of course, fear the golden-winged bird and dread becoming its prey.

There is another story concerning this golden-winged bird. I shall only tell part of the story. Once someone asked a Buddhist teacher, "A bird who has broken through the net—what does he eat?" Such a bird who has broken through the net is perfectly free, being absolute master of himself. We normally find ourselves bound up with all kinds of nets, most of them of our own making. The nets may not actually exist, but we imagine that we are trapped within them. The bird that has broken through the net is a metaphor for the spiritually enlightened person. When the Buddhist teacher was asked what food this bird eats, he was being asked about the kind of life a spiritually enlightened person might lead. What kind of life would a person lead who lives by the Name, who is possessed by Amida? What kind of person would he or she be?

That's the kind of question many of us ask. In fact, most of us or all of us ask that question, although it does not concern us at all. What's the use of trying to know such things instead of *becoming* those things ourselves? Because we are curious by nature, we always try to ask questions which have no relevance to our life. That is the shortcoming of human nature, but at the same time it shows how significantly human life differs from animal life. Animals don't ask such questions.

The master replies to the questioner, "You come

through the net yourself, then I will tell you." When one has "come through the net" there is no need for an answer or a telling. Since he or she knows, there is no need to ask the question, "What would be the life of one who is really spiritually free?" You should free yourself and see what kind of life it is for yourself. In the same vein a person asks, "What is the life of a Shin devotee like?" Or, nowadays Americans often ask, "What significance does the message of Buddha have for our modern life?" Instead of being informed about all the advantages that accrue from the objective viewpoint, you should just accept the Name and try to live it. We might explain all kinds of benefits, all kinds of advantages, material and otherwise, which come from belief in the Name, but it would be meaningless. Instead of trying to understand, just live it. Then you will know what it means.

This is what distinguishes religious life from ordinary worldly life. In the relative life we want to know beforehand all that may come about as the result of doing this or that. Then we make our move, expecting a certain outcome. But in religious life we accept and know and, at the same time, live that which is beyond ordinary knowledge. Thus knowing and living, living becomes knowledge and knowledge becomes living. This is the difference between religious life and worldly life. Yet there is no such thing as spiritual life distinguished from worldly life. Worldly life is spiritual life, and spiritual life is worldly life.

Now, regarding the Name, Shinran states, "Once the Name (*myogo*) is pronounced, that is enough to make you be born in the Pure Land." Birth in the Pure Land is an event that takes place while we are still living in this life.

Oneness of the Name

Recently I was reading a Christian text in which the author spoke about Christ being born in the soul. We generally think that Christ was born on a certain historical date so many chronological years ago, that he was born in a certain part of the world, that he was born by the miraculous power of God and not in the usual way. But this Christian writer states, "Christ is born in our soul, and when we recognize that birth, when we become conscious of Christ's being born within us, that is the time we are saved."[7]

So Christ is born in the course of history, but that historical event really takes place in our own spiritual life. Christ is born when we become conscious of his birth in us. He was not actually born in any specific place, for he is being born in us every day, every minute. He was not born once in history, for his birth is repeated everywhere at every moment. And his birth, this writer says, is dependent on this: the death of all our selfish desires. We must die to what we call evil. When evil is altogether forsaken and the soul is no longer disturbed, there will be no anxiety, no annoyance, no worries whatsoever, for all worries come from our being addicted to the false idea of self. Therefore, when the self is surrendered, all storms are quieted and absolute peace, complete silence, prevails in our soul.

It is wonderful that this Christian writer speaks of silence. When silence prevails in the soul, that is the moment Jesus Christ is born in our soul. So the silence is needed. When everything is kept quiet, the opportunity for spirituality is opened up. Silence is attained when self is given up. When self is given up, the consciousness of duality is altogether unknown.

When I say dualism no longer exists, I do not mean the annihilation of duality itself. Duality is somehow left as it is and yet its two identities are combined. So the two are left as two and yet there is a state of identity between them. Then silence takes place. Duality doesn't simply refer to two, but to the multiplicities in the phenomenal world. When there are multiplicities there are all kinds of noise, all kinds of disturbances.

The noise is eventually silenced, but this silence is not accomplished by the annihilation of multiplicities. The multiplicities are left as they are, yet silence prevails—not underneath, not inside, not outside, but right there. Christ's birth takes place in this kind of silence. The realization of silence is simultaneously the birth of Christ. They occur synchronously.

The Name comes alive in our active life when there is no Name besides Amida. Amida becomes the Name itself, and the Name is none other than Amida. That is the joining of *ho* and *ki*, Amida and each being. In contrast, when the Name is pronounced and we are conscious of saying namu to Amida, or when we think Amida is hearing us calling namu, there is no silence, no true identity. When one is calling out to the other and the other looking down or up, duality exists. This duality means that there is no silence, only disturbance.

But when namu is Amida, Amida is namu. *Ki* is *ho, ho* is *ki*. This is silence. When this silence takes place, when the Name is absolutely identified with Amida, then the Name ceases to be the name of someone who exists outside of the one who calls up that Name. This is perfect identity or absolute identity, but it is not "oneness." When we say "one," we interpret that one numerically, that is, as one standing against two, three, four, and so on. But oneness in the real sense, the absolute sense, cannot be measured, for it goes beyond our capacity for measurement. In this kind of absolute oneness, absolute identity, the Name is Amida, Amida is the Name. There is no separation between the two, *ki* and *ho* are identical.

This absolute faith is reality. This is the moment, as pointed out by Shinran, that if you say NAMU-AMIDA-BUTSU once, it is enough to save you. That the "one" is "absolute one" is a mystery.

4

THE FUTILITY OF PRIDE

Self-Power and Other-Power

L ET US NOW TURN to our discussion of Other-power. Other-power is *tariki* in Japanese, and self-power is *jiriki*. The Pure Land school is known as the Other-power school because it teaches that tariki is most important in attaining birth in the Pure Land, whether understood as regeneration or enlightenment or salvation. Whatever name we may give to the end of our religious efforts, that end comes from Other-power, not from self-power. This is the contention of Shin Buddhists.

Other-power is opposed to what is known in Christian theology as synergism. This means that in the work of salvation a person must do his or her share just as much as God does his. In contrast to synergism, the Shin school may be characterized as monadism, which means working alone in the sense that Other-power works alone, without any self-power being involved. Salvation is all Amida's work. The relative existence which we ordinary people lead has nothing to do with effecting our birth in the Pure Land. Birth in the Pure Land is none other than attaining supreme enlightenment.

What I term monadism, the singular working of Other-power, may be illustrated by the behavior of cats. When the mother cat carries her kittens, she grasps the neck of each kitten with her mouth and carries it from one place to another. That is monadism because the kittens just let their mother carry them. In contrast, monkeys carry their offspring on their backs. This means that the baby monkeys grasp their mother's body with their limbs or tails, so the mother is not doing all the work by herself. The baby monkeys do their share. This is the way of synergism, in contrast to the way of monadism illustrated by the behavior of cats.

In Shin teaching we can say that it is only by the power of Amida that our liberation and freedom are assured. We don't add anything to Amida's working. This doctrine of Other-power, or monadism, is based on the idea that humans are relative beings, and as long as we are so constituted there is nothing in us which enables us to cross the stream of birth and death. Amida comes from the Other Shore, carries us on the ship of the Primal Vow, and delivers us on to the Other Shore.

A deep chasm exists between Amida and ourselves. We are so heavily burdened with karmic hindrances that we cannot shake them off by our own power. Amida must come and help us, extending the arms of help from the other side. This is what is generally taught by Shin people. But from another point of view, unless we exhaust everything we have in our efforts to reach the ultimate end, however ignorant and helpless, we will never be grasped in Amida's arms.

It is all right to say that Other-power does everything by itself. We just let it accomplish its work. Nevertheless, we must become conscious of Other-power doing its work in us. Unless we are conscious of Amida's doing work in us, we shall never be saved. We can never be sure of the fact that we are born in the Pure Land and have attained our enlightenment. To acquire this consciousness, we must exhaust our efforts. Amida may be standing and beckoning us to come to the Other Shore, but we cannot see Amida until we have done all we can do. Self-power is not what is really needed to cross the stream of birth and death, but Amida will extend his helping hand only when we realize that our self-power is of no account.

Since we cannot achieve the end of our endeavors on the path of enlightenment, Amida's help must be recognized. We must become conscious of it. In fact, recognition comes only after we have strained all our efforts in crossing the stream by ourselves. We realize the inefficacy of self-power only when we try to make use of it and are made aware of its worthlessness. Other-power is all-important, but this truth is known only by those who have striven by means of self-power to attempt the impossible.

The realization of the worthlessness of self-power may also be Amida's work. In fact it is, but until we achieve self-awareness we do not realize that Amida has been handling all this for us and in us. Therefore, striving is a prerequisite of any realization. Spiritually speaking, everything is finally from Amida, but we must always remember that we are relative beings. As such, we cannot understand things unless we first try to do our best on this plane of relativity. Crossing from the relative plane to the absolute plane of Other-power may be logically impossible, but it appears to be impossible only before we have tried everything on this plane.

Beyond Self-Power

We have been discussing self-power, the relative plane, devoted striving, and using up ourselves. These are all referring to the same thing, what is called in Japanese *hakarai*, "calculation." This technical term, well known to Shin people, is similar to the Christian notion of pride. Generally speaking, Christians do not use philosophical terms such as self-power and Other-power, but "pride" is none other than self-power. This pride is self-assertion, complimenting oneself as being worthy, someone who can accomplish great things. To rely on self-power is pride, and such pride is very difficult to uproot, as is the belief in self-power.

In our world of relativity our every action depends on self-power. On the moral plane, especially, we talk constantly about individual responsibility, personal choices, and decision making—all products of self-power. As long as we live in a moral world, each person must be responsible for his or her actions. If we acted without any sense of responsibility, society would be really chaotic and fall into demise. Therefore, self-power or pride is needed in this normal world of relativity. This holds true as long as life proceeds smoothly, that is, without encountering any obstacles or anything that frustrates our ambitions and goals. But as soon as we encounter an obstruction in our path, we are forced to reflect upon ourselves and assess our powers.

Such obstructions in life may be enormous, not only individually but collectively. As our society becomes more and more complex, the hindrances and obstructions also become increasingly collective in nature and people feel less and less responsible for them. But whether individuals are conscious or not, when we speak of society—whether a community, a congregation, or a gathering of any kind—each person has to become responsible to a greater or lesser degree if any meaningful solution is to be found.

When we encounter difficult problems, we reflect upon ourselves and find that we are altogether impotent to overcome them. If we did not have any obstacles confronting us, things might proceed smoothly and safely. But the very moment we encounter an obstacle that seems insurmountable, we reflect and find our self-power completely inadequate to cope with the overwhelming difficulties. We then feel frustrated, and all kinds of anxiety, uncertainty, fear, and worry begin to multiply. Such feelings, in fact, characterize contemporary life. Pride is curbed at this point. It has to give way to something higher or stronger. Then pride is humiliated. In our relative world, on this plane of contingency, such obstacles are bound to appear as long as we live. They cannot be avoided.

Earlier Buddhists used to say, "Life is suffering, life is pain, and we are compelled to try to escape from it or transcend it, so that we are no longer shackled to birth and death." They used such words as "emancipation, liberation, and escape." Nowadays, instead of such terms we speak of attaining freedom or transcending the world.

This relative world is characterized by all kinds of strivings, and unless we strive we cannot get anything. But once we transcend relativity, striving, self-power, pride, and hakarai, no effort is expended. Self-power is replaced by Other-power, pride by humility. Hakarai is displaced by *jinen-honi*, a crucial term which will be explained shortly. In ordinary discourse the Japanese say, "Anata makase." *Anata* means you, or thou, or the other. *Makase*, to use a Christian phrase, means "Let thy will be done." *Jinen-honi* means, roughly, "entrusting oneself to Other-power," and might also be rendered, "Let thy will be done."

Meaning of No Meaning

Shinran, the founder of the Shin school, spoke about *jinen-honi* as something similar to "Let thy will be done." His discussion is somewhat technical, but I will present his view.[8] According to his exegesis, *ji* is the word for "of itself" or "by itself." It means things as they are. Birth in the Pure Land is not due to the designing of man but to Amida's Primal Vow. *Nen* means "naturally" or "spontaneously." Thus, the phrase means that people are naturally and spontaneously led to be born in the Pure Land.

When I speak of birth in the Pure Land, it should be understood properly. That is, birth in the Pure Land is not an event that occurs after death. The Pure Land is experienced here and now, and we are carrying it with us all the time. In fact, Pure Land is surrounding us everywhere. We become conscious of it, we recognize that Amida has come to help us, after our strivings have been exerted and exhausted. Then jinen-honi takes place. *Honi* means "It is so because it is so."

We cannot give any reason for our being here on earth. Why do we live? The answer necessarily is, "We live because we live." When we try to explain our existence, it inevitably results in a contradiction. We cannot live even for a moment with such a contradiction. Fortunately, however, contradictions do not get the better of us; in fact, we get the better of them.

Jinen-honi, in relation to self-power and Other-power, means that it is in the nature of the power of Amida's vow that we are born in the Pure Land. The way in which Other-power works may be defined as "meaning of no meaning." This appears as a paradox. When we talk about "meaning," we assume the word to signify something, but in religious life "meaning" has no meaning whatsoever. That is to say, its workings are so natural and spontaneous, so effortless and absolutely free, that it works as if it were not working.

Let us now turn to Shinran and see what he says about this naturalness and spontaneity in living. The following passage is paraphrased from the *Letters of Shinran* (see note 8).

In order for the devotee to be saved by Amida and welcomed to the Pure Land through pronouncing the Name, NAMU-AMIDA-BUTSU, in all sincerity, the devotee cannot know what is good or bad for him.

All is left to Amida. This is what I, Shinran, have learned.

What Shinran says here, that all is left to Amida, goes directly against our moral consciousness, what we call conscience. But from the religious point of view what we think is good is not absolutely good and not necessarily good all the time. That which is considered good can turn at any time into its opposite. And what is regarded as bad can turn out to be good. If that is the case, we cannot be the absolute judge of good or evil, morally speaking. When we go beyond such a division by Amida's help, everything is left to Amida's working. When we become conscious of his working in all things, we do not really know what is good or bad, yet whatever we do turns out to be good. This is a paradox which is inexplicable as long as we live on the conventional plane of morality. It goes beyond our normal powers of comprehension.

Shinran continues, "Amida's vow is meant to make us all attain supreme Buddhahood." As I said before, when supreme enlightenment is attained we realize the presence of the Pure Land, that we are right in the middle of the Pure Land. When we realize the supreme Buddhahood, which is the same as supreme enlightenment, we find that we are in the Pure Land itself.

"Now," Shinran goes on, "Buddha is formless, and because of formlessness he is known all by himself." All physical objects have form, and all ideas possess designation, but when Buddhists talk about formlessness, they are not referring to physical or ideational content. Rather, they are talking about a formlessness which goes beyond the materiality of things and our habits of intellectualizing. In this sense, "formlessness" is uniquely a Buddhist term. That which is formless is *jinen*, "being-by-itselfness." If Amida had a form, he would not be called the supreme Tathagata or supreme Buddha. To suggest this formlessness, he is called Amida.

When we have understood all this, we need not be concerned with defining *jinen* any longer. This is important. When we realize that we are really living in the world of formlessness, we have no more need of talking about jinen, being-by-itselfness.

Shinran continues his discourse, "When you turn your attention to it, the meaningless meaning assumes a meaning that defeats its own purpose." When we talk at length about "being by itself," we no longer are "being by itself." There is no more meaningless meaning. Meaning now has some meaning. It points to something else. But when we become meaning itself, we need not talk about meaning anymore.

When we become jinen there will be no discussion, because we have become jinen itself. All kinds of troubles arise in our trying to figure out what jinen is like. When we begin to think, we find numerous difficulties; but when there is no need to think, everything is all right. We remain human and yet we become like the lilies of the field and the fowls of the air.

Shinran says all this comes from Buddha's *jnana* or *prajna*. These may be translated as "Buddha-wisdom" or "Buddha-discernment." It is that Other-power which transcends our relative way of thinking. While "Other-power" is a dynamic expression, "Buddha-wisdom" is more dialectical or metaphysical; but they both go beyond our relative way of thinking. From Shinran's commentary on jinen honi, we can see what understanding Shinran had of the working of Amida's vow.

"Meaning of no meaning" or "meaningless meaning" may be seen as making no literal sense, lacking any definite content whereby we might grasp its significance. In ordinary discourse "meaningless meaning" is just that—it is really meaningless and has no significance for our life. But the actual idea of meaningless meaning is this: there was no teleological or eschatological intention on the part of Amida when he made the forty-eight vows. Everything expressed in them was the spontaneous outflow of his great infinite compassion, his great compassionate heart, embracing everything and extending to the farthest ends of the universe. This infinite compassion is Amida himself. Amida has no ulterior motive; he simply sees our sufferings and seeks to end them. Amida's vows are the spontaneous expression of his love and compassion, saving us from undergoing the endless cycle of birth and death.

It may sound strange to hear that one can go beyond teleology or live in purposelessness. Everything we do in life has a purpose, but in the religious realm we become conscious of realizing purposelessness, going beyond teleology, meaningless meaning, and meaning itself. This is another mark of faith, stating "Let thy will be done," whereby we let go of self-power and let Amida do his work through us and in us. For this reason there is no prayer in the conventional sense in Buddhism. When we pray to acquire something, we will never get it. When we pray for nothing, we gain everything.

Issa and Eckhart

During the Tokugawa period (1600–1868), there was a poet called Issa in Japan.[9] Issa was noted for his haiku, the shortest form of Japanese poetry, which is limited to seventeen syllables. Issa expressed in this verse form a variation of "Let thy will be done." But in his case it is not overtly religious. In fact, he was deeply involved with worldly affairs and once, not knowing what to do, wrote this haiku out of frustration. I still remember that, when I was young, we paid off all of our bills to tradespeople at the end of the year. In those days, in fact, it was twice a year when all bills were paid, once in July and the rest at the end of the year. If we couldn't pay off the debts in the middle of July, we left it until the end of the year. And if we could not pay, we just went broke. Issa was in just such a predicament:

> Trusting the Buddha, good and bad,
> I bid farewell
> To the departing year

> *Nani goto mo*
> *Anata makase no*
> *Toshi no kure*

He was in a terrible impasse. He is saying, "I, being at the end of the year and having no money whatever to pay all my accounts, have no alternative but to let Amida do his will." If Amida could take care of all of Issa's poverty, there would be nothing better in this world, for he was really poor. He was poverty-stricken in more than the

65

worldly sense. Worldly poverty and spiritual poverty—
sometimes they go hand in hand.

Recently, reading Meister Eckhart I found a
story that you might like to hear.[10] A daughter came to
the preaching cloister and asked for Meister Eckhart. The
doorman asked, "Whom shall I announce?"

"I don't know," she said.

"Why don't you know?"

"Because I am neither a girl, nor a woman, nor a
husband, nor a wife, nor a widow, nor a virgin, nor a master, nor a maid, nor a servant."

The doorman went to Meister Eckhart and said,
"Come out here and see the strangest creature you have
ever heard of. Let me go with you, and you should ask,
'Who wants me?' "

Meister Eckhart did so, and she gave the same
reply that she had made to the doorman.

Then Meister Eckhart said, "My dear child, what
you say is right and sensible, but please explain to me
what you mean."

And she replied, "If I were a girl, I should still be
in my first innocence. If I were a woman, I should always
be giving birth in my soul to the eternal world. If I were
a husband, I should put up a stiff resistance to all evil. If
I were a wife, I should keep faith with my dear one whom
I married. If I were a widow, I should be reverently devout. If I were a servant maid, in humility I should count
myself lower than God or any creature. If I were a man-
servant, I should be hard at work, always serving my lord
with my humble whole heart. But since of all of these, I
am not one, I am just a something among somethings,
and so I go."

Then Meister Eckhart went in and said to his students, "It seems to me that I have just listened to the purest person I have ever known."

This story is entitled "Meister Eckhart's Daughter." I have something to add here. This strange daughter said, "Of all these, I am not one." She considered herself uncharacteristic of all those enumerated. They were not doing anything special in a worldly sense, but she injected some spiritual sense in their activity. "If I were a husband," she said, "I should put up a stiff resistance to evil." That statement is made in a worldly sense, but also in a somewhat spiritual sense, I believe. If one is engaged in a spiritual life, there is some end to perform. If you believe in this or that end, if you have some work to accomplish, you will have something. But she says, "Since of all these, I am not one. I am just a something among some things." I wouldn't say this. I would rather say, "I am just a *nothing* among some things and so I go." "So I go" is *jinen-honi*. It is *sono-mama*. It is "Let thy will be done." This, I think, is a very interesting story.

5
EXCELLENCE OF PERSON[11]

Myokonin

L ET US NOW CONSIDER the *myokonin*, a word that designates the most devoted and insightful follower of the Shin teaching. *Myo* means "wonderful," *ko* is "fragrance," and *nin* is "person." Thus, it suggests a person who manifests the wonderful fragrance of spirituality. *Myokonin* is a term used exclusively in Shin Buddhism, and it is not found in other Buddhist traditions.

These followers are distinguished by some outstanding qualities. They are, generally speaking, goodhearted, kindhearted, unworldly, devoted, and with little formal schooling. They know nothing about scholarship and lack any worldly sophistication. Most noteworthy is that they show no acquaintance with Shin Buddhist doctrines. If they were learned or more sophisticated, their expressions would not come so directly from the heart.

Since they are not highly literate, they are not spoiled by worldly things. What they feel comes out untainted by intellection. Their thought is touched by sincerity, and this comes through clearly in their writings. But usually they don't do much writing; instead of writing they act, and their acts are sometimes quite noteworthy.

I remember one example. Most of the large Buddhist temples in Japan are located in Kyoto. In the country about two hundred miles from Kyoto lived a very pious man. One day he heard that a huge fire was burning the head temple to which he belonged. He immediately took a large carpet, soaked it in water, and shook it in the direction of the temple which was supposed to be burning. Now, a small fire can be effectively put out by smothering it with a wet blanket. If it is a big fire, the blanket itself might be consumed. But when this pious man heard about the fire, he could not help going out and committing himself to the stupidest of all possible actions.

When one's thought processes are intellectual and rational, one can immediately see the futility of such an attempt to extinguish a faraway fire. But when there is no such medium of intellection, grief is experienced at once and one instantly responds, "The fire must be put out," especially when the head temple is burning. When this pious man hears the news, his immediate response, without any hesitation and deliberation, is to go out and shake the wet blanket in the direction of the fire.

Such an irrational, impulsive action, from the worldly point of view, is the height of stupidity and absurdity. At the same time, from another point of view that we might call the spiritual, this man's act makes us ponder more deeply. Really stupid? Yes, but also a certain genuineness of heart expresses itself in this act. Immediacy of response, with nothing coming between feeling and action, distinguishes the myokonin of which I speak.

Here is another story from this group of Shin followers. When a man heard noise coming from his yard, he looked out and saw neighborhood boys climbing up one of the fruit trees in the yard, trying to steal some fruits. So he went out into the yard and placed a ladder underneath the boys in the tree. He then quietly returned to his house. Is this not a stupid thing to do? The boys are stealing his fruits, but the owner does not stop them from committing an unlawful act. This man feared that when the children try to come down the tree, nervous about being caught, they might slip and fall, and hurt themselves. His impulse was to prevent them from being injured, not to save his property from thieves. Such an act is characteristic of the myokonin.

Another story is about a myokonin who left many writings. This is rather unusual, since they do not normally commit themselves to writing. Writing requires a processing through the intellect, and when the intellect interposes itself, expressions tend to become warped and insincere. This person, whose name is Saichi, passed away about twenty years ago, shortly after his eightieth year. His profession was making *geta*, a wooden sandal-like footgear. Saichi made use of wood shavings in his workshop, writing down whatever thoughts came to his mind. In the evening he would gather them up and transfer them into notebooks used by school children in those days. Thus, he kept up a kind of religious journal, you might say, for more than twenty years. Saichi began seeking the religious life when he was nineteen years old and spent about thirty years getting to the truth of Shin teaching. His faith was confirmed when he was about fifty years old.

So attaining the truth is no easy task. It is no joke, not just talk to pass the time. It is really serious work. Shin, especially, is more difficult really to understand than other teachings of Buddhism. Although Shin teachers say that it is the easiest way to attain Buddhahood, to my mind it is the most difficult way to attain Buddhahood.

Language and Spirituality

Before returning to Saichi, let me quote from one of the living myokonin. She is an illiterate woman whom I met when I was in Japan a few years ago.[12] Because she does not know how to write, she dictated the poetry in the following two sections to her son who was about to go away. She spoke in short stanzas, like a folk ballad, and told her son to put it into writing. When I saw her, she was about sixty years old.

When this woman first got married, she was somewhat unhappy, I think, according to her story. She used to go to a Buddhist temple nearby and listen to the sermons. When she went to the temple, she tried to keep her mother-in-law from knowing about it. So there must have been some friction between her and the mother-in-law, not between her and her husband. But in the old days in Japan a woman married not only the husband but his whole family. Even today, to a certain extent, the old lady of the house is quite a despot. About fifty years ago this was especially true. This young woman had great trouble for many years until one day she awakened to the truth of the Shin teaching. When her grown son had to leave her to become an apprentice in a larger city, she grieved at parting with him. There was nothing for her to do but to make the son understand and receive what she had already gotten from the teaching. She wanted her son to comprehend the Shin faith which she had embraced. Therefore, she dictated her thoughts to her son, since she could not write them down herself.

Translations, unfortunately, do not carry the strength and subtle shades of meaning of the original. English is a more intellectual language than either Japanese or Chinese. When the Japanese read their own writings, what they understand from these words is not exactly and definitively established. For instance, I read in English some time ago that one of the great Christian mystics said, "God's Isness is my Isness." This is a highly abstract expression. According to the Bible, when God was asked what his name was, he said to Moses, "My name is, 'I am that I am' "—quite an abstract statement. In Japanese or Chinese we would not use such a highly intellectual and abstract phrase.

In Japanese we have personal pronouns corresponding to your "I" or "you," "he" or "she," but in many cases the subject "I" is omitted, or sometimes "you" is dropped. Occasionally, the object is also omitted, and only the middle term, the verb that connects subject and object, expresses a thought. How do we know that the verb expressed belongs to the subject or the object? How do we know what relationship that verb estab-

73

lishes between the two? All such expressions are quite vague, not stated at all. But Japanese liberally use what we call honorifics. By the use of honorifics, we know immediately whether the reference is to "you" or "I." Honorifics are attached not only to nouns but also to verbs.

All this suggests that what is expressed is somewhat imprecise and what we hear is also quite vague, not so specifically defined as it might be in English. But this very vagueness may help in writings on spirituality. Such writings are not so precise and exact as scientific writings. Actually, this vagueness is not really vague. From the intellectual point of view it appears ambiguous, because it is not well defined—subject is not specifically subject, object is not obviously object. But from the spiritual standpoint subject is object and object is subject. This very indefinability, this vague identification, is in a sense more expressive. Sometimes I think Chinese is the language most appropriate to the spiritual life.

Everyday Life and Nembutsu

Now, this is what the woman dictated to her son.

> When I think of it,
> my heart is quickened
> because of my overflowing joy.
> As I am illiterate, I dictate it
> and my son writes it down,
> filled with as much joy as myself.

Since childhood I went to the Buddhist temple,
but I just listened to the sermons
without paying much attention to their content.
Later, however, impelled by my inner anguish,
I started visiting the temple anew.

Certain inner anxiety is needed in religious life. It is a necessary precursor to make one understand and appreciate religious truth. Without any inner anguish, simply listening to sermons, merely reading religious writings, and trying to get something out of them, is futile. Whatever we get is only a superficial shell.

I have found that the more I listen,
the more grateful I feel, indeed, to my Oya-sama.
Such a feeling I've never experienced before.

Not wanting my mother-in-law to know
each time I visited the temple,
I just quietly slipped out of the house.
Nobody knew where I went.
I thought it was all due to my self-power,
that the nembutsu was uttered.
But it was not so, it all came from Other-power.

As I said before, Shin distinguishes between self-power and Other-power. Self-power corresponds to Christian pride, and Other-power is realized through humility. When self-power or pride is crushed, then one feels humbled, and humility leads to Other-power. Other-power is Oya-sama or Amida or NAMU-AMIDA-BUTSU.

So, whenever self-power is mentioned, that refers to pride. This is what is suggested when this woman says, "I thought it was all due to my self-power."

Everything comes from the power of Oya-sama. This is what distinguishes Shin from many other teachings. When self-power is abandoned, when pride is effaced, it is not due to a person's effort or power. It is all due to Other-power. In order to be really humble and feel humility, we are apt to think that we must get rid of pride and work at being humble. Even though we might think that this is done by Other-power, in the meanwhile we strive with self-power. When we think it is all from Other-power, that very consciousness proves that it comes from self-power.

Other-power actually comes quite unawares and unexpectedly to our mind. When we really have Other-power, it takes complete possession of our consciousness, and self-power goes away altogether. You might ask, what makes us recognize that power as Other-power, when it occupies the whole field of consciousness? In fact, we are not even conscious of Other-power, for Other-power prevails and nothing stands against it. All this defies linguistic description.

Other-power is there, and I am conscious of it, yet that Other-power identifies all my consciousness as itself. I am there just the same. I am I. The Other is other. Yet there is consciousness which cannot be expressed. When expressed, it becomes an absurdity. So, Other-power must be personally realized. This woman really understood Other-power. She continues and says,

> What I was imagining to be Other-power
> was none other than self-power.

> Trying to avoid the path of evil
> and constantly seeking the Pure Land,
> this thought too was nothing but self-power.

Here we find the essence of religious experience. As long as we try to avoid evil and long for the Pure Land, or have anxieties about our birth in the Pure Land, or think that we must abandon self-power, we are in the realm of self-power. That is why myokonin especially ignore the distinction between relative good and bad. They are on the other side of moral thinking.

Religious life always goes beyond moral thinking. This does not mean that religious life is entirely separated, sharply distinguished from moral life. It is true that the religious life is attained by transcending the moral life. But this does not negate the moral life. In fact, the spiritual is contained within the moral, but moral life alone does not reach the religious, spiritual life. As long as we try to reach the spiritual through morality, we are using self-power, and that must be purged. But trying to get rid of self-power is also self-power. One may then ask in despair, "What am I to do?" That is the real question, and it is an impasse through which we all must pass.

Living with Amida

The woman continues:

> I have been designing all the time,
> saying, "Is this the way or that?"

> But there was no designing after all.
> All was given fully and freely by Oya-sama.
> How grateful I am now! NAMU-AMIDA-BUTSU.

"Designing," or *hakarai*, is calculation, human motivation, or effort. Saying, "Is this the way, is that the way?" and "What should I do?"—that is designing; that is moral effort.

It is not quite accurate to say that we should get rid of all these things. To think along such lines is to commit ourselves to the working of self-power. This is the most difficult point. But this unlettered woman fully understood, when she admits, "I have been designing all along, saying 'Is this the way or that?' But there was no designing after all. All was given fully and freely by Oya-sama. How grateful I am now!" And she goes on:

> Because of my blindness and powerlessness,
> the dawn came upon me through the power of
> Oya-sama.
> How grateful I am now! NAMU-AMIDA-BUTSU.

And this dawn, something breaking up or coming forth from an unknown region when we are desperate and in utter despair, when we do not know what to do, causes the light to flash through our minds.

> I was utterly blind and did not know it.
> How shameful to have thought I was all right.
> I thought the nembutsu I uttered was my own,
> but it was not; it was Amida's call.
> How grateful, indeed, I am. NAMU-AMIDA-BUTSU.
> Now that I am convinced of my being

definitely destined for the path leading to hell,
neither the Pure Land nor the evil path is of any use
    to me.

As long as we are relative beings, we are all definitely destined for what Buddhists call the evil path, and we can never escape it. But even as we are destined for the evil path, and may be living in the evil path, we are right in the middle of the Pure Land. When this is realized, we can answer in the way this woman does. For her, neither the Pure Land nor hell, not even purgatory, whatever that is, is of any use. She is now above the Pure Land. She is above the evil path or hell. She then concludes her thoughts:

To whom do I owe my present state of mind?
To the founder, Shinran, and to his successor, Rennyo.
Being taught by these spiritual leaders,
I have now come to this realization.
My knowledge has come through all the good teachers
who have successfully transmitted this teaching.
How praiseworthy they all are! NAMU-AMIDA-BUTSU.
While worrying over my daily life,
fretting about things wanted and wanting,
I am all the time in company with Amida himself.
How grateful I am! NAMU-AMIDA-BUTSU.

Everyday life is of course full of worries, anxieties, and fears. We are living uneasily in the middle of all these troubles, whereas such difficulties do not affect the myokonin at all. They have all the ordinary problems we have, but they are not so bound up with them as we are.

Although they are not free from wants and fears, at the same time they are not bound by them—they are capable of freeing themselves. Though bound, yet they are free. That is what the woman means when she says, "I am all the time in company with Amida himself." If she did not have anxieties, fears, and worries, she could never say, ". . . all the time in company with Amida." This is the most important and significant part, and all religious experiences, all religious teachings, point to this fact. In the woman's words, "Though in parental relationship with Amida, I cannot avoid being bothered with evil thoughts from time to time."

We often think that saintly people are so sublime that they are entirely devoid of evil feelings we generally have. But this is not so. If we were to praise a saint for being free from all worldly things, the saint would no doubt say, "What are you talking about? I am just as bad as you are. And yet," he would add, "I have something which makes me, in spite of all these evil thoughts, free from them and in company with God (or Amida)." The woman's confession continues:

Though in parental relationship with Amida,
I cannot help from time to time
being bothered with evil thoughts.
How shameful indeed! NAMU-AMIDA-BUTSU.
No matter how hard I try not to have them,
they crowd into my mind in ever greater numbers.
What a shame, indeed! NAMU-AMIDA-BUTSU.
Looking at my evil self,
I realize what a deplorable thing it is.
I am disgusted with this dear ego.
How shameful! Truly I am an old hag, a disgusting evil.

But she is ever with Oya-sama who refuses to part with her. She is evil, a sinful person; she is most disgusting to herself, but Oya-sama never leaves her. Oya-sama refuses to part with her.

> Day in and day out I am with Amida.
> Let the sun set whenever it pleases.
> How grateful I am! NAMU-AMIDA-BUTSU.

To "let the sun set whenever it pleases" means this: whenever the time comes, I am ready to die. When the sun sets, when my life comes to an end, I am ready to part with it, and I do not care where I go.

> My time is always passed with Amida,
> no matter how unexpectedly the sun may set.
> How grateful I am! NAMU-AMIDA-BUTSU.
> Praise and reverence is the favor I am granted,
> NAMU-AMIDA-BUTSU.

What a fine declaration of Shin faith and Buddhist understanding! Intellectually speaking, if one is in company with Amida all the time and conscious of the presence of Other-power, how could one possibly entertain or harbor evil thoughts or feel disgusted with oneself? This is reason questioning religious faith. The problem of intellection is its inability to deal with ambiguity and contradiction, which take place in life all the time. In spite of such contradictions, the myokonin are thankful and joyful for what they have experienced.

When pride is gone, there is humility. And humility is recognition of Other-power. When humility is realized, we have a wonderful feeling of joy. Logically, humility should make one feel quite miserable. Yes, it does. But simultaneously one senses a feeling quite opposite to that of misery. In fact, there is joy and there is happiness. Now let us return, after this lengthy detour, to Saichi and his journals.

Embraced by NAMU-AMIDA-BUTSU

Saichi warns us not to give up our joyous feeling, for joy is the emotion that assures or confirms our faith in the Shin teaching. Joy is sometimes quite precious and precarious, so you have to guard it all the time. Saichi questions himself in his writing occasionally, but then adds quite frequently, "Oh, Saichi, how fortunate! No worry, no fretting, no saying the nembutsu."

This last point is significant, because Shin people are supposed to say the nembutsu all the time. Once our faith is confirmed, all the nembutsu you say after that express your gratitude. But when you visit a Shin temple, where so many people are constantly uttering NAMU-AMIDA-BUTSU, you wonder how many devoted followers are gathered there. In fact, what they are saying might be called empty nembutsu, for there may be no feeling at all in it. Listen to what Saichi says about this:

> I don't say any nembutsu.
> It is not necessary.
> Saved by the Buddha's compassion,
> how grateful I feel.

As for NAMU-AMIDA-BUTSU,
it is ever with me.
I am ever with it.
While asleep, NAMU-AMIDA-BUTSU.
While awake, NAMU-AMIDA-BUTSU.
While walking or resting,
while sitting or lying, NAMU-AMIDA-BUTSU.
While working, NAMU-AMIDA-BUTSU.

In one of the songs that he hums while making the geta-footgear, he writes, "Footgear is joy, Saichi's joy. NAMU-AMIDA-BUTSU." This is quite significant. In factories, increasing production is talked about constantly. But all the articles produced by workers and by machines are not accompanied by the sense of joy that Saichi feels in making geta. The result of his work shares and participates in his feeling of joy. The geta-footgear is a symbol of joy. One feels joy not only in making geta, but also in making tables, fashioning lamps, building houses, paving streets, driving a car or bus. All is joy. Everything participates in this feeling of boundless joy.

On the management level, people are always quarreling. I can't say who is wrong or who is right. Perhaps both are on the wrong side. But if all could have this feeling that what we make embodies our feelings of joy, happiness, and gratitude, then the whole world would change into a house of joyousness. Then all work would be joy. While keeping the accounts, NAMU-AMIDA-BUTSU. From within, whatever things I am engaged in, NAMU-AMIDA-BUTSU rushes out. When feeling ashamed of my wretched self, NAMU-AMIDA-BUTSU, and my wretchedness turns into blessedness. When joyous over the Buddha's compassion, NAMU-AMIDA-BUTSU. When feeling sadness, NAMU-AMIDA-BUTSU. When happy, NAMU-AMIDA-BUTSU. Everything turns into the Name, NAMU-AMIDA-BUTSU.

Somewhere Saichi says, "Everything is not only my mind, which is filled up with so many evil thoughts. This mind, with all its evil thoughts, is brimming with NAMU-AMIDA-BUTSU." The objective world is something quite beyond our control. This objective world, according to Saichi, is filled with NAMU-AMIDA-BUTSU. Also the empty space, as it extends beyond the horizon and to the heavens, is itself filled with NAMU-AMIDA-BUTSU. Therefore, everything the myokonin touches, everything he does, everything he says, is NAMU-AMIDA-BUTSU.

In this case, NAMU-AMIDA-BUTSU is no longer the simple adoration, "I take refuge in Amida Buddha." Such a phrase seems to have no intimate pure content, no meaning, no special significance, no symbolic sense. It is simply NAMU-AMIDA-BUTSU, simple reality. Of course, when we say "reality," we are already verging on abstraction. Just saying NAMU-AMIDA-BUTSU itself, with no explanation, is very much better.

This is the essence of Shin teaching, as I understand it. We might say that religious life has nothing to do with our practical life. But in the examples of Saichi and the woman I quoted, we discover how significant religious life can be. It expresses itself in every deed. Christian saints would agree with this. Everything is colored by this religious experience. The world becomes permeated with gratitude and joy. That does not imply that everything bad in life becomes extinct. It is there. It is present and yet it is nonexistent. It is there as if it were nothing. All religious teachings converge on this single point.

NOTES

1. The myokonin are rare Shin faithfuls who manifest their faith in their daily lives, sayings, and reflections. The following definition is from my entry, "Myokonin," in *The Oxford Dictionary of World Religions*, ed. John Bowker (Oxford: Oxford University Press, 1997), p. 671:

> One who practices Shin Buddhism in exemplary fashion and who is likened to a lotus flower. According to Shan-tao (613–81), just as the lotus (*pundarika*) is the most wonderful, superior, rare and unexcelled among flowers, growing out of muddy water, so too is the person who manifests the working of Amida Buddha's true compassion in the midst of a passion-laden world. Biographies of myokonin were first compiled by Gosei (1720–94) and followed by others of Jodo Shinshu tradition. They were relatively un-

known until D. T. Suzuki, the Zen scholar, drew attention to them as exemplifying Japanese spirituality.

Suzuki elaborates on the myokonin in chapter 5 of the present book, "Excellence of Person," but he also writes extensively about them, especially Saichi in his *Mysticism: Christian and Buddhist* (New York: Harper and Brothers, 1956), chapter 10, "From Saichi's Journals," pp. 174–214, and in his *Japanese Spirituality* (Translated by Norman Waddell. Tokyo: Japan Society for the Promotion of Science, 1972), pp. 177–215.

2. For details regarding the combining of the Sanskrit terms, *Amitayus* and *Amitabha*, as well as the origins of Primal Vow and Pure Land, see Fujita Kotatsu's contribution, "Pure Land Buddhism in India," in *The Pure Land Tradition: History and Development*, ed. James Foard, Michael Solomon, and Richard K. Payne (Berkeley Buddhist Studies Series, vol. 3, 1996), pp. 1–42.

3. The forty-eight vows of Dharmakara Bodhisattva appears in the *Larger Sukhavati-vyuha Sutra*. For their translation from the Chinese version that spread in East Asia, see Luis Gomez, *The Land of Bliss: The Paradise of the Buddha of Measureless Light* (Honolulu: University of Hawaii Press; Kyoto: Shinshu Otaniha, 1996), pp. 166–172. All forty-eight vows are called Primal Vows, but usually it is restricted only to the eighteenth vow. Shinran gave his own reading, based on religious insight, of the eighteenth vow, as follows:

> If, when I attain Buddhahood, the sentient be-
> ings of the ten quarters with sincere mind, joy-
> ful trust, and aspiration for birth in my land and
> saying my name perhaps even ten times, should
> not be born there, may I not attain the supreme
> enlightenment. Excluded are those who commit
> the five transgressions and those who slander
> the right dharma.

Shinran interpreted the exclusion clause as an admo-
nition but ultimately saw it as an affirmation of great
compassion that includes the transgressors and slan-
derers in supreme enlightenment.

4. The relationship of *ho* and *ki*, Pure Land and defiled
   land, Namu and Amida-butsu, may appear confusing,
   but they were explained by words and diagrams on
   the blackboard.

5. Shoma, whose dates are unknown, was a favorite of
   Suzuki and is quoted frequently as exhibiting a profound religiosity.

   Meister Eckhart (c. 1260–1327) was a Dominican
   theologian and preacher and a major figure in German
   mysticism. Suzuki used two English translations of
   Eckhart: Raymond Blakney, *Meister Eckhart* (New
   York: Harper and Row, 1941), and Franz Pfeiffer,
   Meister Eckhart, trans. C. de B. Evans (London: John
   M. Watkins, 1924), vols. 1 and 2. See his reference in
   "Meister Eckhart and Buddhism," *Mysticism: Chris-
   tian and Buddhist*, p. 3, footnote.

6. James Bissett Pratt (1875–1944) was a pioneer in religious studies who taught at Williams College. Among
   his works are *The Pilgrimage of Buddhism and a Buddhist Pilgrimage* (New York: Macmillan, 1928), which

contains numerous references to Suzuki. He wrote a
review of Suzuki's *Essays in Zen Buddhism* (London:
Luzac & Co., 1927) in *The Journal of Religion*, 8 (1928):
280–282.

7. References to God born in the soul are found in various sermons and writings of Eckhart. For example,
see the Blakney translation, pp. 103–108.

8. The complete text on *jinen-honi* was translated by Suzuki in his *Mysticism: Christian and Buddhist*, pp. 154–
155. A more current translation from the *Letters of
Shinran*, published by the Hongwanji International
Center, Kyoto (1978), pp. 29–30, is reproduced here:

> As for *jinen*, *ji* means "of itself"—it is not
> through the practicer's calculation; one is made
> to become so.
>
> *Nen* means "one is made to become so"—it
> is not through the practicer's calculation; it is
> through the working of the Vow of Tathagata.
>
> As for *honi*, it means "one is made to be-
> come so through the working of the Vow of Ta-
> thagata." *Honi* means one is made to become
> so (*ni*) by virtue of this dharma (*ho*), being the
> working of the Vow where there is no calcula-
> tion on the part of the practicer.
>
> In short, there is no place at all for the prac-
> ticer's calculation. We are taught, therefore, that
> in Other-power, no selfworking is true working.
>
> *Jinen* means that from the very beginning
> one is made to become so. Amida's Vow is, from
> the very beginning, designed to have each one
> entrust oneself in NAMU-AMIDA-BUTSU and be re-
> ceived in the Pure Land; none of this is through
> the practicer's calculation. Thus there is no
> room for one to be concerned with being good

or bad. This is the meaning of *jinen* as I have
learned it.

This Vow is the Vow to make us all attain
the supreme Buddhahood. The supreme Buddha is formless, and because of being formless
is called *jinen*. When this Buddha is shown as
being with form, it is not called the supreme
nirvana (Buddha). In order to make us realize
that the true Buddha is formless, it is expressly
called Amida Buddha; so I have been taught.

Amida Buddha is the medium through
which we are made to realize *jinen*. After we
have realized that this is the way it is, we should
not be forever talking about *jinen*. If one always
talks about *jinen*, then the truth that Other-
power is not self-working will again become a
problem of self-working. This is the mystery of
the wisdom of Buddhas.

9. The reference to Issa, the Shin priest-poet, is found
in his work *The Year of My Life* (Berkeley: University
of California Press, 1972), pp. 139–149. I quote the
entire chapter to which Suzuki refers:

> Those who insist on salvation by faith and de-
> vote their minds to nothing else, are bound all
> the more firmly by their singlemindedness, and
> fall into the hell of attachment to their own sal-
> vation. Again, those who are passive and stand
> to one side waiting to be saved, consider that
> they are already perfect and rely rather on Bud-
> dha than on themselves to purify their hearts—
> these, too, have failed to find the secret of
> genuine salvation. The question then remains—
> how do we find it? But the answer, fortunately,
> is not difficult.
>
> We should do far better to put this vexing

problem of salvation out of our minds altogether and place our reliance neither on faith nor on personal virtue, but surrender ourselves completely to the will of Buddha. Let him do as he will with us—be it to carry us to heaven or to hell. Herein lies the secret.

Once we have determined on this course, we need care nothing for ourselves. We need no longer ape the busy spider by stretching the web of our desire across the earth, nor emulate the greedy farmer by taking extra water into our own fields at the expense of our neighbors. Moreover, since our minds will be at peace, we need not always be saying our prayers with hollow voice, for we shall be entirely under the benevolent direction of the Buddha.

This is the salvation—this the peace of mind we teach in our religion. Blessed be the name of the Buddha.

Trusting to Buddha
Good and bad,
I bid farewell
To the departing year.

Written this twenty-ninth day of December, in the Second Year of Bunsen (1819), at the age of fifty-seven.

10. This story is quoted almost verbatim from the Blakney translation, pp. 253–254.
11. "Excellence of Person" is an expansion of Suzuki's discussion on the "person" in *Japanese Spirituality*, pp. 75–93.
12. This illiterate woman is identified as Mrs. Hina Mori in Suzuki, *A Miscellany of the Shin Teaching of Buddhism*

(Kyoto: Shinshu Otaniha Shumusho, 1949), pp. 72–74. Her confession of faith is made in verse form in this text, as well as in his *Collected Writings on Shin Buddhism* (Kyoto: Shinshu Otaniha, 1973).

SUGGESTED
READING

D. T. Suzuki wrote many articles and books on Shin Buddhism, and those who are interested in them should turn to the bibliography of his complete works found in *A Zen Life: D. T. Suzuki Remembered*, edited by Masao Abe (New York: Weatherhill, 1986), pp. 235–246. This book includes Suzuki's own autobiographical accounts, as well as approximately twenty articles by Japanese and Westerners on his life and thought.

His primary publications on Shin cited in the Introduction and Notes are the following:

Collected Writings on Shin Buddhism. Kyoto: Shinshu Otaniha, 1973.

Japanese Spirituality. Translated by Norman Waddell. Tokyo: Japan Society for the Promotion of Science, 1972.

Suggested Reading

The Kyogyoshinsho: The Collection of Passages Expounding the True Teaching, Living, Faith and Realization of the Pure Land Way. Translated by D. T. Suzuki. Kyoto: Shinshu Otaniha, 1973.

A Miscellany of the Shin Teaching of Buddhism. Kyoto: Shinshu Otaniha Shumusho, 1949. This is included in its entirety in *Collected Writings*, above.

Mysticism: Christian and Buddhist. New York: Harper and Brothers, 1956.

The original tapes for the present book were edited and expanded into articles that were published in the journal founded by Suzuki, *The Eastern Buddhist* (New Series). Under the title "Shin Buddhism," it appeared in three installments as follows: chapter 1 in vol. 18, no. 1 (spring 1985); chapter 2 in vol. 18, no. 2 (autumn 1985); and chapter 4 in vol. 20, no. 1 (spring 1990).

Readers who wish to know more about the original works of Shinran in English translation should turn to my *River of Fire, River of Water: The Pure Land Tradition of Shin Buddhism* (New York: Doubleday, 1998), which contains a complete list of titles in the endnotes. Written for the general public, the book also incorporates extensive quotations from *Tannisho*, a collection of Shinran's sayings, and attempts to shed light on the nature of all-pervasive compassion that permeates the Buddhist paths, whether Theravada or Mahayana, Vipassana or Tibetan, Zen or Shin. The quotations are from my *Tannisho: A Shin Buddhist Classic*, rev. ed. (Honolulu: Buddhist Studies Center Press, 1996). Beginners should read the afterword before reading the translated text in this second revised edition.

For an overview of the life and thought of Shinran, the founder of Shin Buddhism, readers should consult the standard work by Alfred Bloom, *Shinran's Gospel of Pure Grace* (Phoenix: University of Arizona Press, 1958.) For those who wish to explore the historical background of Pure Land Buddhism, I recommend *The Pure Land Tradition: History and Development*, edited by James Foard, Michael Solomon, and Richard K. Payne and published as the Berkeley Buddhist Studies, vol. 3 (Berkeley Buddhist Studies Series, 1996). Although not a comprehensive survey, it covers important aspects of Pure Land Buddhism, with two chapters on India, four on China, and six on Japan, written by different authors.

The scriptural basis of Pure Land Buddhism is called the Triple Sutras. Two of them are found in *The Land of Bliss: The Paradise of the Buddha of Measureless Light* (Honolulu: University of Hawaii Press; Kyoto: Shinshu Otaniha, 1996), by Luis Gomez. This includes English translations of the Sanskrit and the Chinese versions of the two basic scriptures, the Larger and Smaller Sukhavati-vyuhas. Appendix 3 contains a helpful bibliography, listing all the major works published in Western languages on the Pure Land tradition. The third of the Triple Sutras is *Sutra on the Contemplation on Amida Buddha*, which is probably of Central Asian or Chinese origin. The three are contained together in *The Three Pure Land Sutras*, translated by Hisao Inagaki, and published by Bukkyo Dendo Kyokai (Berkeley: Numata Center for Buddhist Research and Publications, 1995) as vol. 12 (nos. 2, 3, and 4) in their series of translations of the Chinese Buddhist Tripitaka.